Skating Rough Ground

Skating Rough Ground

Poems by

J. S. Absher

© 2022 J. S. Absher. All rights reserved.
This material may not be reproduced in any form, published,
reprinted, recorded, performed, broadcast,
rewritten or redistributed without
the explicit permission of J. S. Absher.
All such actions are strictly prohibited by law.

Cover by Shay Culligan
Cover art by Pedro Sousa, Unsplash.com
Author photo by Tabb Clements

ISBN: 978-1-63980-117-6

Kelsay Books
502 South 1040 East, A-119
American Fork, Utah 84003
Kelsaybooks.com

Dedicated to Patti and John, always present even when absent

> He lifted me out of the miry pit,
> the slimy clay,
> and set my feet on a rock,
> steadied my legs.
> —Psalms 40:3

"The silent world praises and thanks God; man mingles his praise with its. As he gives thanks, he becomes part of the world. But if a man only thanked, he would be swallowed up by the world; he would cease to be man. His voice would be barely audible in the chorus of praise sung by the world. But man is not swallowed up; he is confronted by his need again and again."
—Franz Rosenzweig

Acknowledgments

Many of these poems were written and revised as part of my participation in two poetry critique groups, the Poet Fools and the Black Socks. Special thanks go to Joan Barasovska of the Poet Fools for her careful reading of an earlier version of the book. I would also like to thank two long-time supporters of my poetry—*Visions International,* edited and published by Brad Strahan; and *North Carolina Literary Review,* edited by Margaret Bauer.

Some of the poems have been revised since their first publication.

Agape Review: "Léon Bonnat: *Christ on the Cross* (Paris, 1874)," "Heaven's Gate"

Bay Leaves: "A Good Death," "Closing the Account" (Winner, James Larkin Pearson Free Verse Contest)

BYU Studies Quarterly: "The Creator Praises Birds" (winner, 2018 Clint Larson Poetry Contest), "The Rain on Alan Avenue"

Coastal Shelf: "The Conversation of Matter"

Conte: "Taken"

Dialogue: "Grasshoppers in the Jar of the World," "Until You Come." The four poems published in the section His Own Hand have been selected as the winner of the 2021 *Dialogue* "Bodies of Christ" writing contest and will appear in the Winter 2022 issue.

Grand Little Things: "Ballade of the Top," "Sheol"

Heron Clan VI (anthology): "Thomas Eakins, *Consummatum est* (Philadelphia, 1880)"

Irreantum: "Art," "Thomas Eakins, *Consummatum est* (Philadelphia, 1880)"

Kakalak: "When I have fears …."

North Carolina Literary Review: "Flower of Zeus"; "Gentile Bellini, *John the Baptist* (Istanbul, 1429)"; "How Rhodon the Tutor Prepared Cleopatra's Son"; "In my yard are henbit"; "In the Chapel"; "The Newsy"; and "Weeding"

Pinesong: "Patient John Doe in the Rec Room" (winner 2017 Carol Bessent Hayman Award from the North Carolina Poetry Society); "Sheol"

Rat's Ass Review: "Letters," "Town Boy"

San Pedro River Review: "Full Moon at Fews Ford"

Sunstone: "That's Alright, Mama, Just Anyway You Do"

Third Wednesday: "Clue of Home"; "Dawn and Later"; "I Sing" (selected as Poem of the Week); "Slow" (also selected for public display in the Poetry in Plain Sight program sponsored by the NC Poetry Society)

Visions International: "Chosen," "The Inconvenience," "Time Past and Time to Come"

Webster's Reading Room (Old Mountain Press anthology): "Traveling Inside My Room"

Contents

His Own Hand

Prodigal	15
What the Right Hand Is	16
What the Left Hand Does	17
Fingers	18

The Body Selectric

I Sing	21
Theories of Origin	23
Full Moon at Fews Ford	24
Double Talk	25
Slow	26
Mechanics	27
Ballade of the Top	29
Taken	30
Chosen	34
Grasshoppers in the Jar of the World	35

Interrupted at the Crucifixion

How Rhodon the Tutor Prepared Cleopatra's Son	39
Art	40
The Monks	42
In the Chapel	43
Gentile Bellini, *John the Baptist* (Istanbul, 1479)	45
Léon Bonnat, *Christ on the Cross* (Paris, 1874)	47
Thomas Eakins, *Consummatum est* (Philadelphia, 1880)	48
Edgar Degas, *Little Dancer Aged Fourteen* (1895)	49
The Newsy	53
Each Time I See the Tide	55

Flying Above the Steeple

Children on Mertie Road (1960)	59
Winter Rain Daylong Falling	61
The Day	62
That's Alright, Mama, Just Anyway You Do	63
Town Boy	64
Traveling Inside My Room	65
A Good Death	67
Closing the Account	69
Clue of Home	71
The Conversation of Matter	73

What Sorrel Is For

Weeding	77
Patient John Doe in the Rec Room	78
Time Past and Time to Come	79
Campsis radicans	81
When I have fears…	83
Flower of Zeus	84
Dawn and Later	86
Letters	88
The Direction of Flow	90
In my yard are henbit	91

Holy Commerce

Your Graces and Your Gifts	95
The Inconvenience	96
The Rain on Alan Avenue	97
Sunday Drive	98
When I Go	99

Until You Come	100
Sheol	102
Waiting for Hospice	103
At Heaven's Gate	104
The Creator Praises Birds	106

His Own Hand

"I desire to be to the Eternal Goodness what his own
hand is to a man."
—*Theologica Germanica*

Prodigal

He first clasped the neck of his son in joy,
not grief—the aging father in Rembrandt's
Return—then the shoulder and back of his boy
kneeling, one shoe off, one on. The large hand
on our right, Father's left hand, is the roughened
hand of clenching and judging, the peasant's
who handed his unwomaned queen a gift of snakes.
The hand on our left, smaller for pity's sake,
is feminine and soothing, made to caress.
The big hand is grasping the shoulder in fear
he will lose the boy again; more hopeful, gentler,
the other touches him with lovingkindness.
Return again and be Our sons and daughters,
Yahweh pleads, Return: We will be Father
and Mother. Prodigal says, I am a man:
look at these scars on my hand.

What the Right Hand Is

Part scars and wounds—the index finger crooked
from a long-forgotten break; the dint
where a melon spoon of cells, precancerous,
has been scooped out; the little crescent
moons under each nail, the nails badly bitten;
the worn-out cartilage at the base of the thumb
that ruins my grip and sometimes sleep, when bone
of metacarpal scrapes the trapezium—

it's an old hand, but take it, and all
it screwed in or up, hammered or caressed,
lines botched, weeds pulled, promises kept. Small-
time doer even when it does its best,
it is most itself when, doubled in yours,
it loses half its fear of coming years.

What the Left Hand Does

My hands are taking the years hard.
Item: The left is acting on its own.
Example: As I proof a poem online,
it hovers over the keys, then slowly
descends, wrist relaxes, a fingertip
drops, depressing almost always a *d* or *t,*
plosive consonants that blow up the word
they land on, bomblets from a passing plane.
This is not how I pictured my later years,
worried about an errant hand. *Item:*
When I pass my cluttered desk, how often
it drags off a book or stack of papers.

The left thumb became arthritic first:
that hand lifts and grasps, the doctor said,
its partner finesses. Right has been
the writer since I was young, Left
the written on. At ballgames, the right
goes over the heart, the left dangles. Right
throws, Left wears a glove to catch.
Dexter acts, Sinister suffers. *Item:*
The right waves happily as a child departs,
the left clasps the back of the neck in grief.

Fingers

Just look at them, clumsy claws
that are fat and short, raw
sausages, not digits—spillers,
knockers over, arthritic grippers,
nailhead missers and thread strippers,
packaging grapplers, tyers of shoes
that won't stay tied, slappers
of skeeters, swatters of flies,
typo makers, smearers, droppers
of eggs and messy breakables,
pimple-, bubble-, button poppers,
filchers of river-rounded pebbles
for garden paths, china breakers
and rim chippers, crystal-crackers
(they've cost me dearly), rock skippers,
just once (I swear) bird flippers,
zipper-downers and zipper-uppers,
and takers of the Lord's Supper:

often, too often, have they failed me—
look at the piles of scribbled verse—
but did not punch or thieve or worse,
or do much shameful or barbarous,
unlike the fingers Rodin sculpted
bristly, lurking in the dark,
that (wrote Rilke) seemed to bark
like the five throats of Cerberus.

The Body Selectric

"Have you got some kind of a machine,
an X-ray or a vacuum cleaner maybe that sorts
out the words you want?"
> —Sugarpuss O'Shea, in Charles Brackett and Billy
> Wilder, *Ball of Fire* (Samuel Goldwyn, 1941)

I Sing

the body Selectric
the Royal portable and the Olivetti

their beauty and efficiency
balking account

I sing the Underwood Universal
the platen and the platen knob

poets pecking the keyboard
their necks curved, their heads bent

the words defeating paraphrase
the words per minute whereby hangs a job

the carriage release lever
the feed roller, the ribbon spool

TODAY we are naming
the parts and poems

the smell of machine oil
the clean slap of typeslug

against ribbon and white
twenty-pound paper

against onion skin, against
thicker cream-colored resume stock

dearly bought by the unemployed
the watermark of their desperation

O Optima, o Smith-Corona
o Remington Noiseless Portable in Duotone Green

who knew your day would be so brief
where is the strength

of our finger-joints and our fingers
the vowels typed sweet and clean

the rapidly moving carriage
the bell at the margin

the cramping hands, the jammed keys
of Hermes Baby, of Olympia?

Theories of Origin

Zanzibar, '35—
a little hotel, a patio,
ivory dealers in burnouses,
the barkeep simpatico,
a round on the house,
night and day the phonograph playing
Night & Day
while Porter's in the corner saying
I wrote that in a taxi
in the roar of the traffic—
no, at lunch with the Astor's
in Newport, when it was raining
drip drip drip—but no,
it wasn't so prosaic—
I took the wife (no, lover)
to the starry mosaic
vault of a mausoleum—
no no no, it was the plaintive
cry of the muezzin
from a mosque in Morocco—
and no it doesn't matter
darling where it was
on the Black Sea or a bus's
backseat—doesn't matter
if in a bar in Zanzibar
or on far out Antares
or in patent dancing shoes
under a nightclub moon.

Full Moon at Fews Ford

The river eddies and flowers,
wrinkling into bloom: petal slides
over petal; a fresh rose blooms
as moment shunts into moment,
the new dying as it buds,
the old blossoming as it fades.

When mind is half-asleep, like mist
it drifts formless over the valley
till it meets a crooked sycamore
as white as smoke and turns
back on itself, a wisp of thought
fading as it flowers.

Double Talk

After Rilke, "Abandon entouré d'abandon"

Surrender within surrender,
    letting go inside a letting go,
tenderness caressing tenderness,
    caress tendering caress,

without pause your inner being,
    Psyche without cease
caresses itself, they whisper,
    tenderly strokes itself, they say,

caresses itself within the self,
    interiorly self-caresses,
by its own light illuminated,
    lit by its own reflectiveness.

So you have invented the theme—
    the apt image has come to you:
the answer to Narcissus' prayer
    is the praying of Narcissus.

Slow

We were standing under the bright
bole of the sycamore that split into three
crooked fingers. Even in the noon glow

we could not make out our hearts. *Slow,*
you said, *slow,* and hours dissolved
into the scent of night flowers.

Look, you said. Under the alder,
their wings folded like Dürer's praying hands,
the butterflies waited for light.

Mechanics

The bric-a-brac
of language, plumber's
helper and liquid
plumber, vice

grip, goo
remover, two-part
epoxy glue, octave
and sestet,

high school di-
ploma, biplane
strut, dual over-
head cams:

let it be a little
uneducated,
let it stick and fly
and unclog drains.

Let it stand
in awe when beauty
walks by, Venus
in her cloud—

a glimpse
and she's gone.
Let it grill
steaks. Let it thrill

someone who
picks up a book
and can't let go.
Let it rev and hum

and fit pipes
and glow.

Ballade of the Top

When stuck, be wise and practice the art
of sticking. Endure what must be endured.
Arthritis. Yapping dogs. When heart
or head is scarred,
accept the healing offered. Though hard
to be like the saints who roasted on a griddle
while the executioners cheered,
think long, feel deeply, say little.

Are you a patient waiting to depart
with an unspeakable diagnosis; a bird
snagged in burdock, terminally hurt,
your syrinx too broken to be heard;
a street poet with a beggar's beard,
biting the tongue for fear your own hustle
will con you into passing a bogus word?
Think long, feel deeply, say little.

The good life is a top maker's art:
joy and pain, deliberately blurred,
revolve on one axis, not spheres apart.
Spinning together through the world
they cheer the heart-battered.
Joy dances to the devil's fiddle
and do-si-dos with Jesus. Damned or raptured,
think long, feel deeply, say little.

From judgment and love you are not spared,
nor from solving the ancient riddle—
which are you: lamb redeemed or mutton slaughtered?
Think long, feel deeply, say little.

Taken

i.

Above her,
almost white
sky scalloped
by dark leaves.
The car reeks
of Camels.
Her eyes burn.
If she strains
she can see
above her
a bald crown
wreathed in smoke.
Hands and feet
tied with twine
tingle, throb,
go numb. Her
gagged tongue swells.

She wakes, sees
not a dream
landscape but
headlights' gleam
blazing trees'
low branches.
Will it help
to picture
sky blue eggs
clutched in high
safe places?

To recall
days the air
shaking gold
on parked cars
shone as if
flammable
with grace? When,
if ever,
will You come
rescue me?
Three-in-One,
can I be
whole again?

ii.

God sees what
she cannot—
plexiglass
sheets airborne
from the truck
ahead—how
they plane through
the air, catch
the asphalt
by edge, by
corner, break
into shards
flying back
like arrow

flints piercing
grill and wind-
shield, driver's
skull and chest,
how the car
swerves, catches
a guardrail
head on, guts
itself, how
she is thrown,
swaddled with
cord, into
unplanned birth.

iii.

Every birth
is unplanned
by the born,
a rich gift
they could not
request, but
must return
on demand.
She flew, not
knowing why,
from fire, from
crushed metal,
to laurel,
shattered limbs
in a fall
of cupped blooms,

lay flowered
on the ground
in pink-edged
white, lay bound
to the earth
she had not
yet escaped.

Chosen

An uncanny presence, perhaps an angel, seems to accompany Isaac.
  —A. G. Zornberg, *The Murmuring Deep*

When Rebecca first sees Isaac, she falls
from her camel. *Who is that man?* she asks,
*that stranger alone in a field
who wounds me like this?*

> She covers her face with a veil. Not now,
> but soon as yesterday, she'll ask, *Why me?*

What Isaac is doing in the field, no one knows—
the Hebrew verb occurs nowhere else. Translators
improvise: he's *strolling*, or *languishing,*
or *meditating*. Then he lifts up his eyes.

> He is conversing with his angel
> who says, *Lift up your eyes,*

just as Rebecca's whispers, *Take that
loitering man: his angel stopped a father's knife.*
The fate of Esau, red as a bean and hungry,
already is stewing; already

> his mother-to-be is going to cheat him
> out of what he'll have traded away already:

Choose the son who wrestles with God and lives,
her angel will whisper, veiling the old man's
eyes with a sheepskin scrabbled
with dark words. Choosing, we are chosen.

> *Why me?* she asked when the nations
> were scuffling in her womb: *Why me?*

Grasshoppers in the Jar of the World

The jar is silent because it is full of praise.
The grasshoppers are loud because they, too,
brim with praise, clicking as they fly.

The grasshoppers jump, but the jar is too high.
They try to climb, but it is slippery,
and clicking they slide and fall, slide and fall.

Why does it need sides if the jar is all?
If there's nothing else, why should the grasshoppers
want to fly away? If they are not machined

to take it on the lam, why bother with legs and wings?
The jar is silent because it is full of praise;
the grasshoppers click, praising as they fly

the outside because it is outside,
because it is unknown and out of reach,
because it makes me them angels of desire.

Interrupted at the Crucifixion

"Among those killed [during Genghis Khan's raid on Nishapur] was an old man in his library who did not raise his head from prostration when the Mongol soldiers barged in."
—Musharraf Ali Farooqi

How Rhodon the Tutor Prepared Cleopatra's Son

Caesarion has a belt he loves—Cavafy
will describe its rows of amethysts and sapphires—
and obeys his tutor while traipsing dominions
of waste and sea to exceed Octavian's grasp.

Form: hexameters. *Theme:* a king's power. *Governing
image:* snow. *Questions for thought:* in the Delta's heat,
did your mother while still a child ever conceive
snow's possibility? When history cold-shouldered

her to Ephesus, where it chilled her spicy wine
with last year's ice; when it unrolled her from a rug
in a little avalanche, and then dispatched her
into the beds of Roman studs, her melting point

lowered by ambition; when it brought her to Rome
blazing, mistress of Caesar in his last winter,
to melt her sweetness into the boiling Tiber
and to raise you, dear boy, to lead *Res Publica,*

did she ever see it fall, or hold out her hand
palm up like a child to catch and see it vanish,
or watch its slow white liquefaction on the down
of bare arms, setting goose-bump legions on parade,

or roll it into a man that, like Anthony
when the nations were burning, could not hold his shape
but flowed unmanned away? *Process:* Collect your thoughts
and images, arrange them neatly, end on this

moral: snow that lingers on field and forest kills,
but dissolved in spring heat gives life. *Application:*
like a fistful of snow in summer's hot dry mouth,
little Caesars must melt to give Augustus life.

Art

is not (our docent says)
pictures composed of pure
bloodless light. No, it is

the generations of masters
who labored on this icon
to wrest heavenly glory

from hammered metals
and pigments of earth.
It is the young woman

who hid Madonna and Child
in the swaddling of her sack,
the commissar who shot her.

(Our docent, lifting
his shaking hand, points
to the next icon.)

See what craft can do
when acid bites
into copper,

etching the crushed
fronds of fern
under the dying virgin's head

in such fine detail
the mortal pain becomes
a mordant beauty.

Observe the flurry of hatching
around her staring eyes,
and the object of their gaze—

a flowering thistle,
emblem of wounding
and punishment

that bristles in the sun,
each hair casting
its tiny scar of shade.

The Monks

The night the monks rampaged,
drunk in love for their savior,
they toppled the immense
statue of Zeus Diupater

crying, Wake! Wake from sleep!
Blindingly pure and woke,
they sliced the throats of the priest
and his children, and broke

into a thousand pieces
a famous brazen heifer
so lifelike men once tried
to drive her to pasture.

In the Chapel

In the Capilla de la Grenada
an elegant poet with a blood-red
carnation in his narrow lapel,
vade mecum in hand, is looking
at the bridle of the Cid's horse
and, beyond, at *Lagarto,*
the stuffed crocodile sent
to Alfonso the Learnéd. It seems
to float in the air. In its mouth
(he reads) was once a scroll
from the Mamluk Sultan of Egypt
asking for Alfonso's daughter—
her hand, it read, synecdoche
for the pleasures of her body,
her breeding capacity, wealth
and connections, as the crocodile
had in its own time joined
in the marriage of the belly
a harem of hands and feet
both Coptic and Muslim. *Poor
Lagarto,* he writes, *you thought
none could leash you or jimmy
the doors of your mouth.* It's 1260
Christian time.

Alfonso's eligible daughter,
Berengaria, is not quite seven.
Her fiancé has just died;
his father, a French Louis,
has sent a regretful note
stained with dynastic tears.
The Sultan, fresh from the glory
of routing the Mongols, is murdered
by an even more glorious man

whose enemies cry out,
Would that we were dust!
Later, when Berengaria
abandons court for an abbey,
she'll rule still, with free hand,
as Lady of Guadalajara,
her body and her land.
Power—the last desideratum,
the turner of phrases
who has so little and wants less
is writing in the flyleaf,
You are our Lord, Lagarto*:*
empty-mouthed and empty-bellied,
you stretch over vacant space
and hang upon nothing.

Gentile Bellini, *John the Baptist* (Istanbul, 1479)

Art cannot save us, the docent says
    to the no one listening
(emperor and clown, lover and priest
pay him no mind): but what fool would say
it's worth it to be saved without art?

When Gentile Bellini painted
    the Baptist's unshouldered head
(he says), the blood at the cut bubbled
and winked, mimicking *utile et
dulce* the executioner's art.

But when he showed his royal patron
    the deft product of his hand
(the dark prison, the tumbled body,
Salome's décolletage), Mehmet,
his eye practiced in the ruler's arts,

objected, *I admire the brushwork
    and coloring—they make me
half in love with death. But see—his nail
gouging the painted wound—see how his
neck protrudes? It should contract: the art

of the slaughtered body is one I've
    mastered by repetition.*
Mehmet dragged in a slave, a man who
once had sung for him in full-throated
ease. *What can you do for him with art?*

He commanded the Jew's beheading.
   Maestro, paint—and paint quickly:
how well you catch the exquisite fast-
fading violet! To cut throats, fast,
before they slice yours—that, too, is art.

Léon Bonnat, *Christ on the Cross* (Paris, 1874)

Is death, posed, worth more than an artless life? The question
    troubles the art student; she
ransacks memory, old crow inspecting a corpse:
    God, disease and history
endow the artist with the eye of *memento
    mori,* with income enough
from dead soldiers and crow-pecked proles to fund any
    taste—a lesson of the caws
    in Père Lachaise, lost on Bonnat,

for he fetched from the *salle de dissection* a corpse
    dead of indecipherable
causes and nailed him to a cross, eager to glimpse
    how a thin man of Adam
is altered by crucifixion, how a nameless
    dead *clochard* becomes lucid
for us, his suffering at last inescapable
    of notice, on the edge of
    the circle of our attention.

Thomas Eakins, *Consummatum est* (Philadelphia, 1880)

Eakins had worked all day, so of course he felt crossed
    when interrupted at his crucifixion.
Inspired by his old teacher, Bonnat, he had gone
    into the Jersey woods to raise a cross;
his student, Wallace, had put on the crown of thorns,
    disrobed like a swimmer, backstroked up the Rood.
Hunters blundering in profaned the moment.
    He packed up, went back to Philly. The Bloody Tree

rose bloodless on his roof. Wallace re-ascended, the painter
    painted, dogs barked, neighbors were indifferent to the cross—
and it is finished. No one buys it. The priests he lends it to
    hide it behind a door; the knob pokes a wound, x-shaped,
into his canvas with no pierced side, no flowing blood, no halo
    or darkened sky. Who for such a device will live or die?

Edgar Degas, *Little Dancer Aged Fourteen* (1895)

1.

Zoé keeps house and reads to Degas
from his favorite anti-Semitic paper.
(I am pained by this but tell it true.)

All day he has made and unmade clay figures
with the rapt and knowing hands
that feed and clean himself.

Tonight he'll sleep on the studio floor,
amid fragments of dancers and a horse's leg,
sour bathrobes, a zinc tub, easels

displaying contorted women
in charcoal, the teeth in one fist combing
the thick hair gripped in the other,

and his *danseuse* modeled in wax
and plasticine, her secret body
(an x-ray reveals)

of paintbrush handles, wood
shavings, cotton rags, and cork
stoppers—detritus

of art and life, where he will make
his bed tonight, where Zoé
is forbidden to clean.

2.

The *petite danseuse,* creature
of beeswax and clay
enclosed in a glass case

like millinery—she will watch him sleep.
He learned to model the little body
of Marie von Goethem

when his sight was failing. He ran
the eyes of his hands over the muscles
and joints of the ballet rat

willing to pose nude, for four francs
(negotiated by her mother, who had three
more daughters and herself to market)

contracted to stand all day in the fourth
position, her proportions measured
by the old man with his pointed tool

like Blake's God on his knees compassing
the void, her "arm from shoulder to wrist
2 heads in length," wrote Degas;

to be vaguely seen and sharply felt,
nude and clothed, posed and re-posed;
to endure weeks of the ill-tempered old man

who did not care to possess her
as artists used to possess their models,
but only to re-make her on a cross-

piece of metal, a wire mesh, her body
like ours filled with the random
stuff of living, her eyes almost closed,

her wax chin thrust forward, leek-
green ribbons around her neck
and gathering her hair.

3.

Little Marie, fired by the Opera
for missing practice to pose
for easier money, disappeared,

and slipped, too, from the artist's mind
in the way he abandoned a piece
once hands had rendered its truth.

The smaller-than-life version pondered
how to escape. She almost got away,
in '81, the one time she was shown.

But the ugly things they said!
She was a "flower of the gutter,"
her face a "plebeian muzzle"—

a monkey's, said Parisians—her
features deformed by Degas (some
thought) into the "physiognomy

of a whore," the right leg
stretched out unnaturally long
to give grace to her resting position.

He gave her the ugliness without which,
he said, is no salvation. Was it
for this fierce craft

his Jewish friends, some of them, forgave
the "monster of intelligence, terribly
dark, prodigiously bitter"? I have tried

to shape him almost true. He said
a landscape is a state of eyes.
The dancer is a state of hands.

The Newsy

Fantasia on a photograph by Vivian Maier, March 1954

Give him a lonely heart.
—The Chordettes, *Mr. Sandman*, 1954

The man in the box—a wooden shed—
sleeps. Dark brimmed hat, dark overcoat,
a light shirt with a dirty cuff exposed
at one wrist. He leans towards *Horror
(Tales of)*, the "man-eating death flower,"
towards *Beetle Bailey* and *Bozo*,

away from "McCarthy's Men" Schine
and Cohn (their dirty cuffs about
to be exposed), away from *House Beautiful*.
The newsy sleeps in his wooden stand,
beneath his naked light; behind him his
radio sh-booms, rain or shine;

below him *Life*, below *Life* "Terror
Pl..." on the front page of the *New York W....,*
the headline masked by Emperor penguin
and fuzzy chick. *New Yorkers* look down on him;
he looks down on "New York's commie cop"; above,
Wedding Bells hangs by a clothes pin:

an unbride's tears ("I can't hurt Mother,
try to understand") fall towards Hepburn's
gamine bangs, her pain-concealing
smile: Father left, then Hitler kissed her
mother, a secret she'll die with: "I can't
expose her. Try to understand."

It's a night for fantasy. Lights smear
the high glass across the street;
a man trudges away from us, bent
over an out-of-sight dolly. Did he buy
or filch *Il Progresso* to take to Mama,
stealthily lift a copy or leave five cents

for the newsy in his wooden room,
dreaming beneath a naked bulb?
His radio, rain or shine, sh-booms.
Here Mama, maybe says the dolly man,
didn't I say I'd never return to you
even from hell with empty hands?

Somewhere Cohn, too, is dreaming: his
lonesome nights are over; he tells it
to the daffodils. He walks through
a good house: here the mother adores
the son, there the family feasts
on under-the-table deals, behind that door

the maid does laundry and the reds
are sorted out. He too, will be sorted
and remaindered, pulped and shunned.
Like every mother's child of us, he'll burn
with the acid words he slings on others.
Love could be a dream. Try to understand.

Each Time I See the Tide

We passed the time away, Boone is singing,
and as he sings I watch our babysitter.
He is *writing love letters in the sand*
as she jots the lyrics down on notepaper.
She lowers the needle into the groove, listens
a moment, lifts the needle to write,
How you laughed when I cried, then carefully
sets the needle back on the 45.

I am six. It is summer. She is wearing
pedal pushers, says memory (it sometimes lies).
I'll lose everything else I know about her,
except her devotion: sixty-odd years later,
I capture what I recall—how she writes
the crooner's words about vanishing letters.
She doesn't know she's writing them for me
to save a childhood moment from erasure.

Flying Above the Steeple

"Was it not a kind of doom that the ancient gods, no less
than the demons, were subject to—the deprivation
of the power to commit suicide?"
—Miguel de Unamuno, *Tragic Sense of Life*

Children on Mertie Road (1960)

Moses and Noah were standing in the garden;
the boy saw their robes of bright petunias.
(The skin of heaven wore thin above the mountains:
the sacred could seep through like strained milk.)
The girl sat reading the encyclopedia
to get at the birds and bees. By her feet

Uncle was watching her hair—it reached her feet,
almost—silkier than corn silks in the garden
and flowing past the encyclopedia
down to the wilted handfuls of blue petunias
he'd brought her like a child. Her skin was milk
and red delicious. His was leathered. A mountain

stood over the house—a hill they called mountain—
and it gave them fire and honey. The four feet
of Noah and Moses were sour as curdled milk
where the boy saw them sprouting in the garden
like mushrooms among the clumps of brindled petunias.
The girl was eating the encyclopedia

down to the seedy core. Encyclopedia
volumes were heaped up in her room, a mountain
stained with fossils of dried and pressed petunias.
Uncle set marbles and lost keys at her feet
then lay down in the patch they called a garden
and gazed through space with eyes as mild as milk.

When Daddy brought home the bucket of warm milk,
the girl put down the encyclopedia,
the prophets took to wing and fled the garden.
The boy could hear their cawing on the mountain.
The children heard Daddy's red-winged muddy feet
champ like brinded cattle through the petunias

into the house, a skin of broken petunias
on each boot toe. He strained the Jersey's milk,
made the children wash their dirty feet
and put on shelves the encyclopedias
and Uncle's pretties. *There's fog upon the mountain.*
A spate of rain is coming. He stood in the garden

on steel-toed feet. The encyclopedia
had nothing on bruised petunias, or the sweet milky
mountain, or smoke rings blooming in the garden.

Winter Rain Daylong Falling

I sit in the dark recalling Memaw's chinquapins
poured from a paper sack and heaped on her lap.
She culled the wormy nuts and told me stories.

We sat in the light of the store's big window,
in the light of her smile, beside a silent Philco,
Paris, Moscow and Chungking on the dial.

Later she gave me a book on the war called Great,
the boys in Belleau Wood falling in the wheat,
her name on the flyleaf penciled "Sallye,"

and an interlinear "pony" of the Gallic Wars
to ride out Caesar's prose ("he did see a battle to be-
about-to-be") during her year at Glade Valley.

It must have hurt to cull the chinquapins, to clothespin
shirts and strain the milk and string the beans
and roll out biscuits with fingers stiff as claws—

not that I thought then much about it, but when
I did, at 12, I quit picking the berries, quit churning
the butter, quit running about the loveless house

on errands too painful for her legs and feet,
quit because I could not bear her hands' and feet's
deformities, when they most needed my legs and love—

before the strokes, before her speech was gone,
before the three pigs (going to the fair
to trick the wolf) and the wolf too were gone.

The Day

The little room's only window looked out
towards the ridgetop, the Dunkard church in the curve
of the two-lane, and, just beyond, the graveyard.

The morning sun sidled in past the partly
closed slats and resolved into rays and flecks
burning in the light—dust motes, I know,

and likely knew then, too, but still I watched
entranced one morning after our breakfast.
On this day I'd have otherwise forgotten,

probably my grannies were in the kitchen—
Emma with arms stretched out to read who'd died
(she'd be in the Dunkard cemetery soon),

half-crippled Sallie stringing the green beans
(years of suffering and strokes lay just ahead)—
while I stood quietly in the little room

watching the random sparkles in the sunbeam,
worlds I could move with a single breath
of poem or prayer, but could not control.

That's Alright, Mama, Just Anyway You Do

Mama said she just had to see Elvis
as he traveled back to Memphis by whistle-stop:
He'll be something, she sighed, *in his dress blues.*
Daddy said, *No,* with a look in his eye,
so she didn't. But he did, and brought back news:

*Though Elvis never opened his mouth, the town
shouted and clapped and laughed and snapped their Brownies.
A reporter said we were cheering his army buddy
while Elvis was holed up in his private car
shooting craps.* Now everyone, from the muddy

banks of the Holston to the Chilhowie Road,
for a moment longed to live bigger, even Daddy.
The men thought and tried to grow rich, took
Carnegie, won friends, invested as friends advised,
but lost their shirts and nerve. They tried to shuck

the littleness from the little, not knowing all
salvation comes of being kind and small.
The wives had cosmic Jesus and "Don't be Cruel"
to play on their forty-fives and dance. They puffed
their Luckies and they kicked off their dime-store mules.

After Elvis left, Mama slept in. She dreamed
her thin voice soared over his aching growl.
As the stripes turned to feathers on his sleeve,
they flew above a steeple, singing duets—
like angels, Mama dreamed, and half-believed.

Town Boy

One summer evening, '59 or '60,
we drove down ridge and hollow
on dirt and gravel roads, past a stand
of silking corn in a narrow meadow,
through fields of Holstein cattle,
to a milking barn and a tumble-
down smokehouse and a pale white silo,
a steeple without the bell.

At last we came to a dirt-gray
clapboard house. Boys with dirty nails
and a naked baseball welcomed me to play
with my soft town hands. The farmer,
smiling but gaunt, the mother,
with the cracked still beautiful

sugar bowl of her mother, laid
chores aside to be hospitable.
One of their milkers had died;
they took us to the barn to see her butchered.
They pulled back ribs and hide
like heavy curtains, sliced open the belly
and unexpectedly I saw the calf inside her,
its hairless milky skin, its hooves like curds.

They worked by a hissing, flickering light.
We watched from the shadows till it was late
and the cow was nothing but cuts and waste.
They gave us a quarter-side, said, Come back soon,
and waved us home into a low whey moon,
our faces lit up by the green dash lights.

Traveling Inside My Room

I heard the children playing in the town pool.
From across the street and down a steep bank,
their laughter rose up to tempt me, along with
their tinny music, diminished with the distance

like a tall boat on the horizon shrunk to nothing.
I was on my bed, window open, reading—
Gulliver was waking to find himself
staked under a burning sun, his clothing

and hair knotted to fine strings, the strings pegged
to the ground by tiny people with tiny
voices, like a tin-can telephone's. I wanted
to splash and tan in the sun, but, even more,

to be rescued from the weak and small, that
first summer I stayed inside my head.

****

That book, and others, we'd found in the house
when we moved in. It was signed in a neat
round hand on the flyleaf *Nathan B.*, a man
who'd killed himself and left his sister alone.

You can read books and do yourself in. Or not
read them, and do the same. I own his *The Light
that Failed* and his sister's college annual
from '22, when Billy Sunday came

and preached the Book, and maybe saved her
from what her brother did. Or made her laugh.
I own a book of poems Daddy annotated
in the months before he did himself in.

I dog-ear pages and scribble notes. Dear book,
they promise, someday I'm coming back to you.

A Good Death

Fall 1977

I take my yellow pad and felt pen.
They've told me not to come to work again.
Your nerves are shot, they say. *Get some help.*
But they're afraid I'll talk. And I'm afraid,

sure they've bugged the house. Again
the do-re-mi in my head, as I slide
out of my car, wondering how I got here,
on the ridge I'm walking up, thinking

of the old man who could stand at the top
and see nothing he didn't own but sky. Too tight
to spend his cash on fire, Jones wore his coat
indoors all winter and ate his supper cold.

I sit on a root and write, conjuring
the old man in his 80's scything grass
with an easy, fluid motion, laying it down
in swatches as neat as a schoolmarm's letters;

the muscles rippling across his back
as he swung the blade; the rhythm he settled into,
paying out no more effort than needed
to finish by dark. I write, *I wish I'd learned*

to die like Jones at harvest, a well-worn
tool in hand, a ripe field beckoning.
Now I'm back in the car, the Fury
starting, the world streaming by like water,

the road beneath my tires turning liquid.
Now I swallow the pills as if I were a child
and they were candy corn—a handful—two handfuls
like shaped notes in the mouth, the darkness

singing fa-sol-la, 'tis eventide,
the stupor will abide with me,
and I know how the dead wake, eating
grains of dirt to get back to the light.

Closing the Account

December 1977

The solstice nears. Slush of old snow funds
the Yadkin with dirty commerce. Clay banks
dictate their depositions to the river.
The river is not satisfied. I write

over each doorway in the house
I'm sorry. I'm sorry. The flamboyance
is for myself, to show God I really
suffer. What is it I've forgotten?

I begin the last words on my pad:
*I rise with dawn and feel like hell.
Voices in my head, voices among
the waking birds, 'Come and see,*

a bushel of barley for a penny.'
They led me like a child through court
to testify against my kind, my friends
from childhood. I did it for my children,

to look them in the eye. As my sole
bargaining chip with God. I've blazed all
the lintels with black magic marker,
but the angel will not pass over.

Pill bottles by the bed, in the library
a rack of guns. But this is how it ought
to end: like cut grass, blanched. Like morning glory
shriveling to a pin. What will the milk cow do?

Go on chewing what she has chewed before,
her milk vein swelling to feed her bag.
Cast into the fire, I will smoke like fat.
The world we love will go on being the world.

Clue of Home

May 2020

> *You think it is the bird which is free. Wrong: it is the flower.*
> —Reb Zale

For the first time in weeks I walk out
towards our ponds, now dull as muddy boots,
but in high summer the slime algae
will conjure a bright green. The mulberries
are pale, the mock strawberries blood red.

On the banks are yellow irises, oxalis
leaves as purple as old bruises, blooms
the white of clean bandages. Catchweed
ramps beside me, reaching out to grab
my pants-leg and go places.

But I don't go far or often. I read and watch.
In a show I'm binging, an L. A. detective
looks for a spent slug by raking detritus
aside with his foot. When he walks behind
the warty bark of a tree, I wonder, *Our*

hackberry or a lookalike? Memory goes
to places I've been, the once ordinary
rhythms of life, a family I visited
when I was 10—their almost cool, dew-
wet mornings and muggy afternoons,

the June bug's leg they tethered to a thread
while it tried to fly home, the buzz
of its little engine overrevving.
I too was homesick, in agony,
especially the clammy nights.

In the harbor, near mothballed Liberties,
the father snagged a jellyfish with a stick,
pulled it out of the water and held it high,
a snotty handkerchief. I wanted to go home,
if home is the place you never have to leave.

The Conversation of Matter

I could hear things talk. When something was lost,
I stood in the room, asked it to show itself.
Sometimes it spoke an image in the mind—a drawer
    to search, a cherry
    bureau to look under.

Those who have spent their lives mastering tools
and techniques can hear their material speak,
David crying naked out of Carrara marble
    to be rescued from
    Agostino's botched start.

But things usually speak by resisting—
weight too heavy to lift, edge too sharp to hold,
a moving part that grinds and heats and breaks, a poem's
    application of
    friction to language—

slow it! stoke it hotter than Gehenna!
salt its path with grit! keep it from slip-sliding
away on its own melt! flick sawdust into the eye
    to make it dilate!
    Without friction—so said

Wittgenstein, older and word-worn—language
does no work. If it wears skates on rough ground, it
takes a tumble. Even prayer needs resistance—a stick
    crosswise in the throat
    garbling words like a sob.

How hard to admit we love the world—how
hard it ought to be—yet its unrequiting
beauty resists abandonment: *Show yourself, come out
    of hiding, come out
    of quarantine, and live.*

What Sorrel Is For

"Let no smallness retard thee;...if thou beest not Cedar to help towards a palace, yet thou art a shrub to shelter a lamb, or to feed a bird, or thou art a plantane to ease a child's smart, or a grass to cure a sick dog."
—John Donne, *Essays in Divinity*

Weeding

On all fours, I pull the wood sorrel
from the creeping jenny. Experts say
you can never get all its rhizomes and runners.

You'll be on hands and knees every day,
they mean, and I won't mind
so long as I can get back on my feet.

Sorrel means *sour,* not the bright
chestnut of the horse. *Jenny* comes from
chinny, for "chin cough" (we call it *whooping*),

and was used as a specific, not because
it worked, but because they had to try something
to keep the graveyards from filling with babies.

Everything with a name has a history
and a use. Soapwort. Purslane. Eat it, clean with it,
use it for ground cover. Use it for metaphor—

history, the thuggish rhizome in our garden.
We creep on all fours trying to remove it,
but it always comes back

and we somehow manage always
to get back up again—not all of us, I mean,
but some. Sorrel is for sorrow.

Patient John Doe in the Rec Room

Doe recalls a question Buzurjumihr
put to Aristotle: What is love?
Love is a pearl, he answered; lovers are divers.
But divers, adds Doe, who become mangled

in the sea's indifferent machinery.
Eyes shut, lips sealed, Doe is at a table
half-listening to a half-hearted argument,
I couldn't care less versus *I could.* Someone

is talking in a low voice, fast. *I drove to the mall,*
she says, *drove there myself, I could do
that then, and I parked, and I walked in, and
the parking lot was so hot my shoes*

*sank into the asphalt, and I went where I always went,
to watch the ceiling fans turn, seven clockwise,
five counter, while the breeze was cooling
my face, and people related to people I'm not*

*related to were strolling by. If all at once
the fans swooped down with the blades still turning,
I wondered would our heads roll through the store
thumpety-thump.* No one seems to be listening,

except Doe, who could care less and who remembers
another question posed by Buzurjumihr:
how should we think about ourselves in the world?
But the fast-talking woman is back in the car

driving fast, windows down, hair streaming.
I don't know where I'm going, she says, *can't
remember where I've been.* Like a traveler, thinks
Doe; so Aristotle answered Buzurjumihr.

Time Past and Time to Come

The present is a cow grazing
the meadow—a fawn-colored Jersey,
from muzzle to switch absorbed
in filling her rumen. Many cattle,
many presents, moving together
across the meadow to the hill,
up the hill into a stand of locusts.
They graze and chew, passing the world
through four stomachs beautifully
named by those who left nothing
but words behind them, their "great
and solemn consolation": omasum
that some call manyplies,
abomasum, the honey-combed
reticulum, the paunch.
The cattle leave their pasts
behind, in dark green puddles.

And that's what time is, or so
said the boy, or would have said
had he had more years and words.
But the man who stood him a beer
was holding forth. Time can be bought
and sold, he said, like everything,
up to and including God.

First we told it by breath and pulse.
Time was our own, the height
of the sun just where we stood.
The cheap clock we wound and set
three times a week spilled time
like a drunk, then mopped it up
like a long-suffering wife.

Hours expanded, a bear's paunch
stuffed to bursting with berries and grubs,
or shrank to nothing, sifting
and hissing through sleety days.
The salesman liked to talk, liked better
to watch people listen to him talk.

But now time moves by wire,
telegraphed from the central office,
distributed like bread or beer
from a loaded wagon. Carried by signals
that cleverly account for the time
of transmission, it is networked, franchised,
traded and sold, punched in, punched out—
all the time in the world to make
wheels and cogs dance dawn to dawn,
shifts to start promptly, salesmen
from distant provinces to meet
for drinks in Rome at straight up noon.

Son, he said, these days, that's what time is.

Campsis radicans

Consider my vine,
    says the Lord,
how its tendrils
    creep up your house
and snake through
    gaps in clapboard
and floor. Cut it
    to the ground,
it resurrects;
    dose it with poison
and salts, its runners tough
    as the devil's shoestring
send up sprouts as tall
    as July corn and tassel
out in trumpets.

Though I crack
    a pipe to drink, it says,
or break
    a window, or climb
slash pines,
    my blossoms toll
like prayer bells
    and feed the ruby-
throated hummer.
    Children, spend summer
digging and spraying;
    crawl crabwise
with trowel and clippers
    sprout to sprout
cutting and cursing me.

*When the sky is low
and rain freezes to road
   and wire, you will share
my dream:
   fingers will pry out
window-frames,
   pull down a chimney and kindle
the broken fireplace
   with gilded petals.*

When I have fears…

A friend found Solon weeping for his dead son.
'Why do you weep?' he asked. 'It cannot help.'
'That is why I weep—because it cannot help.'

I haven't had to cry for my son like that;
I live in the uneasy faith I'll never
have to. But then it will be his part to weep,

and it will not help. Thoughts I forbid myself
keep pushing through the hardpan of denial
and habit. But it's spring now, time for the green

fuse to blow things open, for birds to sing, for
hummers to squabble for sugar water. Nests
are beginning around us, invisible

mostly, though I saw one sparrow trying out
a mophead. We are all but locked down, my son
and I, and everyone else, birds in a cage.

Letters help. I've been reading about Solon,
I'll write, but not his words about comfortless
tears, nor that he battered his head with clenched fists

when he came home from a long journey to hear
of his son's death. Instead I'll write, how evil
those days were: the wise spoke, fools decided.

Flower of Zeus

He had seven thousand sheep, three thousand camels, five hundred yoke of oxen, five hundred donkeys, and very many servants.
—Job 1:1

Trellising the one rose,
admiring the surviving
verbena, deadheading
the marigold, and watering
the solitary peony

and four hellebore, 18
irises, 13 begonias
(in pots and out),
three pansies, spreading
phlox and bugleweed;

caring for one son (far),
one stepson (near),
two elderberries, two
kinds of mint, one
kind wife to cling to

in pain and in peace,
the Holy Spirit—all
cultivated against
ruin and despair:
I ponder that man

who loved his herds and flocks,
his sons and daughters,
secure in his sense
of rightness, of a life
of plenitude and joy.

A single day took it
all from him, by theft
and murder, by fire
from heaven, by a gust
of wind. These days I fear

one microbe, a fearful
cop, an angry canceler's
lust to erase, one moment's
inattention at the wheel
or in a friendship.

In prayers as short
as breath, I offer up
a bleeding heart, crushed
muscadine and pink
dianthus, flower of Zeus:

Purge me from fear
and anger, give me
a cheerful face, a heart
of gladness and tender
mercies, wisdom's beginning.

Dawn and Later

We know not what we should pray for as we ought.
—Romans 8:36

Dawn comes in over the trees
across the lawn through window glass
to illuminate the books in line
at the back edge of my desk.
Its rosy fingers caress
Abba before *Eban,*
the *r* in rainer, *Deli* in
Delighted States, and all
the *Wit* in *Wittgenstein.*

Not that I see it, most
days. I sit out of the sun
so I can read a screen.
If I go into the sun
it's to observe the plants
I've arranged more or less
at random under the trees,
shade and dappled-light
lovers—mints and cleavers,

begonia and impatiens.
They hold still, inviting
contemplation. They come back
every year, even some annuals—
persistence is a neglected
virtue—and all they ask
is water in drought, weeding,
vigilance against pests,
the occasional feeding.

After noon, I stand among them
hearing leaves stir, and, over
the din of traffic three blocks
away, the distant snare drums
of a marching band. What
should I wish for, I wonder;
which prayers will touch
heaven? I wait to be told, needing
so little, wanting so much.

Letters

I don't like long phone calls, long
texts even less. I don't care for most
long poems. But I do enjoy my son's
five-page letters—sometimes printed
from his desktop, more often handwritten
in neat cursive, without strikethroughs,
erasures, or insertions. He drafts them
in pencil, deletes, interpolates,
then makes a clean copy. His long
walks. His progress in German. Office
politics. His ink is a dark sky blue.

We write intermittently, sometimes
ping-ponging our deepest worries.
Once, years ago, I took him with me
to the finance company to take out
a loan; I wondered if he sensed
the humiliation I felt for putting
the little we had up for collateral,
the cheap stereo, the mattress
on the floor we shared, little else.
I don't ask; he probably doesn't
remember. A lot goes unmentioned

in any relationship—some things
don't need to be said, others can't.
At 70 I may not live to tell all
I ought—too many second thoughts,
too many hard fact-checks against pride
and compassion; and if the past holds true,

poems I'm starting now will survive me
undone. Dear Son, it will not be
cause for grief: the world is never finished.
The sky, this early afternoon, ten days
before Christmas, shines bright blue.

The Direction of Flow

The low sun picks out
the crushed glass in the pavement.
It sparkles like little stars
in the darkness of the asphalt.

I walk downhill past a house
of imminent death: the woman
who lives there, always
a little aloof in her faith—

but not too much to work
the thrift shop at her church
or help me with my flowers
or tell me which neighbors

are lonely or sick—is flowing
darkness to light. The glass
in our roadway once let
sunlight through, held amber

waves of whiskey, hot tungsten
filaments, cold bread and butter
pickles. I walk on down the street,
past the mulberry, to the pond

almost black in this light,
not a patch of sky reflected
from where I stand. It is hard
to imagine absence. Home again,

I make soup for the neighbor's
husband—a doer not a thinker,
but he is learning patience. My pansies
flower yellow for the New Year.

In my yard are henbit

henbit but not henbane
chickweed and henbit but not hens-and-chicks
and here wild mustard and muscadine
fat hen and chick wittles and henbit again
(it is edible and everywhere and unobtrusive)
and bee-beloved abelia (not yet in bloom) and black cherry

sorrow for ingratitude (a small red bloom)
azalea showily in front of the house
mayapple and pawpaw modestly in back
a few more chances to do things right
(they bear large white blossoms)
begonia and rock foil and stonecrop

and debts incurred to dirt and rain and sun
one rose, wild blackberries its cousin
evening fears and morning's graces (also cousins)
phlox and foxglove
unpayable debts to the lord
of hellebore and dogwood and bleeding-heart

two weeks after Easter, 2018

Holy Commerce

"The language of repentance is not a kind of bubble
on the surface of things."
—D. M. MacKinnon, *A Study in Ethical Theory*

Your Graces and Your Gifts

I see now how I limited my life—
saw a milk cow slaughtered, but did not
use a knife; yes, I did kill a snake,
but weakly, with a gun; did not skin
    the rabbit, but I ate.

Twice I worked with a car repo man,
Marine vet, service revolver under the seat:
he faced the deadbeats down and took the keys.
He died of a wound from the war
    I lucked out of.

I taught a young teacher from the Sudan
some dance steps, but never saw her again. Planted
tobacco but didn't smoke. Loved my daddy
but love couldn't save him. Dressed two
    corpses for resurrection.

Packed in a crowd at the Forbidden City,
I was bodily picked up and helplessly moved
several inches. Always carried—by loving wife,
quorums of doubting believers, siblings and friends,
    even rank strangers—

so I learned grace. Did not bleed in the garden,
did not ascend the tree. If I have laid
my hands on others to bestow a blessing,
I spoke—I tried to speak—only the words
    I was given.

The Inconvenience

The window is open just enough to let in the cool night air.
I'm mourning the death of the death of God—
He totes a valise and takes up a lot of room

and has come back like the bird that used to visit:
every evening for a week she hovered above the blooms,
the window just open enough to let in the cool night air.

She looked in at me, curious, even judgmental, as I was writing,
then—pfft! gone! forgotten after a day! But suddenly one evening,
maneuvering through a *valse* as showy as ostrich plumes,

she came back. He's like that, too, suddenly back, the bastard,
with all his baggage. He's packed enough for a millennium
in that portmanteau of his. It takes up a lot of room

(it's as big as an empty coffin), slides the laptop off the table,
shoves the divan till it dents the drywall, pushes my poems
out the window I cracked open to let in the cool night air.

He will take a lot of management. I'll have to humor him,
find somewhere to stow his valise bulging with ostrich plumes.
For God's sake, he tells me—I mean Mine, he says—
      get a bigger room,
and a floor-to-ceiling window to let in the cool night air.

The Rain on Alan Avenue

How the Missionaries Came to Marion, Virginia, 1955

In that far year when I was a child
(you were not yet), I saw how rain
on long afternoons can chitter and chat,
gurgling and chortling out the downspout,
its sing-song tune boring a brat
with nothing to do.

That was the winter rain made us slip
and slop through mud, and noses drip,
till April drizzle made way for the sun.
The roadside rocks were slickered with light
and cherry trees rose out of the dark
chemised in white.

That year heaven made constant noise—
ice that sizzled in the pale beech leaves,
blackberry hail that rattled the roof,
the high fall wind (it made trees bow
till they licked the ground) with a whirring voice
repent, rejoice;

and boys in the street going two by two
wearing snow-white blooms *Good morning* said
to Sister Rain in the leaf-choked gutters,
Good morning, brother, to Mr. Brown
at the window pane who reversed his frown
and said, *How do.*

Sunday Drive

In the shadow of the guard rails, the unmelted
ribbon of snow unspooling for miles. *All
our weaknesses can kill,* the radio preacher
says, *but one will finally get us.* It's cold,
but the sun glows, smoky torch of winter.
The iced-over snow is sweating. I wonder
which weakness will nail me.

> *Buddy, make me a pallet soft and low,*
> the man at the intersection is singing,
> *I'm broke and got nowhere to go.*

In the median, the skin and bone
of naked crepe myrtles. Heaven's this way—
an almost empty road, a guardrail for safety,
a thread of cold that stitches us to the wounded
world. *Kiss Jesus' feet,* the preacher exhorts.
Embrace me, says everything. Clouds
unstring their icy pearls.

> The man at the intersection shakes with cold.
> He has dropped his white bucket on the snow.
> *My lips are blue,* he says, *warm them on yours.*

When I Go

by the path to the river,
in the coil of shadow
space and time
will prestidigitate
out of a sleeve
a ribbon, a slithering
of hard muscle
that will lie in wait.
I will fear its eyes
lidded with copper,
and from my stash
of venom and love
I would pay
whatever it asks
to slide down the bank
and cross safely over.
But it will not budge
while I stand still,
and I cannot cross
until it makes its move.
Over there, something
like Wisdom or Finality
is waving. It wants to clasp
my hand, to tell me
secrets—why the blazing
infinitude of stars
turns blue in the river,
how from the empty
top hat of space
voilà! emerges the grace
to outwait anything
merely human.

Until You Come

Taipei, '97. I walk past side-street
vendors selling lychee nuts and black
rice cakes, to an acre of bare dirt,
concrete pylons lifting a cloverleaf.
A grizzled man by a beat-up Buick
throws gobbets of meat from the trunk
to a growling scrum of gaunt,
scruff-biting dogs, their flying spit
bright yellow in the headlamp.
They've waited days for this.
I turn back before they see me,
dogs or man, fearful I've seen
things I shouldn't.

Cherbourg, '71. Hair cut short, shirts
bleached white, with copies
of Mormon's *Book,* we reach
the lone house facing a field
where the North Sea rigs are being built,
on the paved yard a graying woman
and her mewling, hissing cats
hunkered head down by lumps of flesh.

Five years since I came here,
the woman says, *in answer
to a classified, to help madame
tend these cats. She disappeared,
left me a car, this house, a note—
'Look after* mes minous, *I'll
be back.' No, not interested
in your religion, unless it'll
help me eat as well
as these cats.* Hard to swallow
the bread of patience,

the salt of courage. *Bye-bye*
(she dismisses us in English),
tell Maman *you've met*
the viceroy of the absent.

And now it's me who's gray
and waiting,
at times almost undone,
having neglected nearly all
I should have tended:

undo me further
till I am wrecked, not
man or mammal,
bird or insect, but
elemental,

till You come to heal
or break.

Sheol

I shall discover forever my own absence
—Dilys Laing, *The Collected Poems*

It's damp, but not from weather;
half-dark, but not from night:
like the blue-green jars in my cellar
brimming with dust and dim light
that wait for summer to fill their bellies
with peaches bright as yolks pickled
in vinegar and cloves, with red jellies,
with honey from sourwood and thistle,

I, too, wait in a twilit space
emptied of what I was and said,
of how I did and was done to.
When will I be filled with grace
and all the lonesome laid-out dead
be summoned to come to?

Waiting for Hospice

In his battered pickup he drives to the scrapyard,
on the days he can breathe. The rest he spends in bed
alone. He faces his last days, each one hard.

He is unsistered, he is almost unbrothered.
The father that riveted them together is dead.
The 93 S-10 he drives to the scrapyard

is loaded with brake rotors, A/C coils, yard
and dumpster jetsam, and the cast-iron dread
of being alone on his last days, each one hard.

He knows too many nurses, ER and heart
and lung. None ask, *My dear, are you afraid?*
In his rusty pickup he drives to the scrapyard

wheezing and dizzy, hauling off our discards
to buy his smokes. Friends help with rent and bread
and laugh with him, easing his days, each hard.

The hope of seeing his father is his hole card.
Other hopes got off their haunches and strayed.
In his pickup he drives himself to the scrapyard
alone, facing his last days, each one hard.

At Heaven's Gate

When avid divas and tonsured primates,
evangelical David's psalming
before the Lord, gandy dancers straight
time rain or shine paid weekly, fray-cuffed
clerks, grads of Princeton and Barbizon
Beauty, horse-, brew- and web masters,
    sad copy writers

open wallet and purse; empty out their
fanny- and back-packs; divest brief- and
make-up cases; stave in casks; crack wall-
safes, rifle thumb drives; in dying loose
the colon, taste the bile in the duct,
salt tears in the lacrimal gland,
    the dry mouth's last spit,

God will say, No, not enough: as He pulls
worm segments from hens' gullets, and from
rumens the cud, so from us He'll draw
compassion from the belly's inward
parts, a burning light from our pitch-dark
performances; from grave and urn
    remake broken lives

until lies are untold, the murdered re-
born, the stolen restored, regretted
days made holy as sun-drenched Sabbaths,
grieving parents comforted, *amor*
always *fidelis,* false gods' falser
politicos rejected, our
    weaknesses transformed

praising His name, and even envy weeps
in joy of it all—the night settling
in, the mallards sleeping on one leg,
the drone of semis climbing the grade
out of town hauling repentant prayers,
the freight of our holy commerce
    too massive for words.

The Creator Praises Birds

Vent and crissum,
lores and crest and comb: I
made them all—the

nares, nape, those
horny bill plates—I in
feathered trochees

made them: peacock,
sparrow, tufted titmouse,
flitting jenny

filled with joy of
beaking worm, of strut and
glide, of piping

double on their
syrinx. Praise how flock and
murmuration

call out warning,
call to fly or roost or
call for pleasure:

See me! Hear me!
Pur-ty! Pur-ty! Pur-ty!
Cheer up! Pibbity!

Praise the brave-heart
tender fledgling, wobbly
winging over

houses, over
pavement, risking all to
climb the air by

beating wind I
too created, rising
heavenward in joy.

Notes

Epigraph from Rosenzweig: *Understanding the Sick and the Healthy*, cited by Avivah Gottlieb Zornberg, *The Murmuring Deep*, 2009.

His Own Hand:
    Epigraph: Quoted in William James, *The Varieties of Religious Experiences*, 1902.
    "Fingers": Rilke is quoted in Diane Ackerman, *A Natural History of the Senses*, 1990.

"Theories of Origin": "In 1935 Cole Porter experienced what he called 'the greatest surprise I ever had' when, arriving in Zanzibar, he went to a little hotel with a patio, and 'all these ivory dealers from East Africa were sitting around in their burnouses and listening to "Night and Day" being played on an ancient phonograph.'"—William McBrien, *Cole Porter*, 1998.

"Grasshoppers in the Jar of the World": Inspired by a passage in Zornberg, *The Murmuring Deep*: "[T]he Tower of Babel narrative …. takes its place in a field of midrashic imagery that is haunted by the mythic terror of slipping and falling. In one sinister metaphor, grasshoppers in a jar try in turn to climb out, only to fall back into the jar."

Interrupted at the Crucifixion: The epigraph is from "Magic Lantern: Genghis Khan and the pharmacist-poet's soup bowl" (8 December 2013), http://www.dawn.com/news/1061282.

"The Monks"—Inspired by a passage in Ernst Robert Curtius, *European Literature and the Latin Middle Ages*, 1948, on the period after Christianity became the state religion: "Hordes of monks travel through the land … destroying works of art. They are followed by … vagabonds hungry for booty, eager to plunder villages suspected of impiety." In the Greek Anthology, a series of poems celebrates the lifelike sculptures of Myron (ca. 480–440 BC).

"Léon Bonnat, *Christ on the Cross* (Paris, 1874)": *Clochard* is a tramp or vagrant.

"Thomas Eakins, *Consummatum est* (Philadelphia, 1880)": *Consummatum est,* it is finished," is from the Vulgate translation of the Gospel of John 19:30—"When Jesus therefore had received the vinegar, he said, It is finished: and he bowed his head, and gave up the ghost."

"Edgar Degas, *Little Dancer Aged Fourteen* (1895)": The poem is deeply indebted to Camille Laurens, *Little Dancer Aged Fourteen* (Other Press, 2017). The quotation near the end is a paraphrase of Paul Valéry.

"The Newsy": For the photograph, see http://www.vivianmaier.com/gallery/street-1/#slide-40.

"Flying Above the Steeple": The epigraph is from the translation by J. E. Crawford Flitch, *Project Gutenberg EBook of Tragic Sense of Life.*

"Winter Rain Daylong Falling": "He did see a battle to be-about-to-be"—literal translation of *videbat proelium fore* from *Commentaries of Caesar on the Gallic War,* Book I, 1893.

"Time Past and Time to Come": The quotation is from Elias Canetti, *The Agony of Flies,* 1992.

Holy Commerce: The epigraph is quoted by Geoffrey Hill. "The Lords of Limit," *Collected Critical Writings* (Kindle Locations 138–140). Kindle Edition.

"Your Graces and Your Gifts": "bleed in the garden"—Luke 22:44.

"Until You Come": *mes minous*—my kittycats

About the Author

J. S. Absher is a poet, editor, and independent scholar. His first full-length book of poetry, *Mouth Work* (St. Andrews University Press) won the 2015 Lena Shull Competition of the North Carolina Poetry Society. Chapbooks are *Night Weather* (Cynosura, 2010) and *The Burial of Anyce Shepherd* (Main Street Rag Publications, 2006). His poems have appeared in numerous journals, including *Dialogue, Irreantum, North Carolina Literary Review, San Pedro River Review, Tar River Poetry,* and *Visions International.* In 2018 he won the Larson Poetry Prize from *BYU Studies Quarterly.*

He is preparing three books on North Carolina and southern history. The first two, *Love Letters of a Mississippi Lawyer* and *My Own Life, or The Deserted Wife,* were published in 2021. He lives in Raleigh, North Carolina, with his wife, Patti.

www.ingramcontent.com/pod-product-compliance
Lightning Source LLC
Chambersburg PA
CBHW070548090426
42735CB00013B/3115